XTREME MOMENTS IN SPORTS

BASKETBALL

A&D Xtreme
BOLD HI-LO NONFICTION

An imprint of Abdo Publishing
abdobooks.com

ALEX MONNIG

TAKE IT TO THE XTREME!

GET READY FOR AN EXTREME ADVENTURE!
THE PAGES OF THIS BOOK WILL TAKE YOU INTO
THE THRILLING WORLD OF BASKETBALL.
WHEN YOU HAVE FINISHED READING THIS BOOK, TAKE THE
XTREME CHALLENGE ON PAGE 45 ABOUT WHAT YOU'VE LEARNED!

ABDOBOOKS.COM

Published by Abdo Publishing, a division of ABDO, PO Box 398166, Minneapolis, Minnesota 55439. Copyright © 2023 by Abdo Consulting Group, Inc. International copyrights reserved in all countries. No part of this book may be reproduced in any form without written permission from the publisher. A&D Xtreme™ is a trademark and logo of Abdo Publishing.

Printed in China

102022
012023

THIS BOOK CONTAINS RECYCLED MATERIALS

Design: Series Designer Kelly Doudna, Mighty Media, Inc.
Production: Mighty Media, Inc.
Editor: Liz Salzmann
Cover Photograph: Fred Jewell/AP Images
Interior Photographs: Amy Sancetta/AP Images, p. 30; Anonymous/AP Images, p. 16; AP Images, pp. 10–11, 12–13, 17; BETH A. KEISER/AP Images, pp. 22–23; Brocreative/Shutterstock Images, p. 44; Carol Francavilla/AP Images, p. 21; Chris O'Meara/AP Images, p. 20; DAMIAN DOVARGANES/AP Images, p. 28; David Longstreath/AP Images, pp. 18–19; DOUGLAS C. PIZAC/AP Images, pp. 24–25; Eric Risberg/AP Images, pp. 38–39; Erik Drost/Flickr, pp. 34–35; FabrikaSimf/Shutterstock Images, p. 1; JACK SMITH/AP Images, pp. 26–27; Jim Mone/AP Images, pp. 42–43; Lorie Shaull/Flickr, pp. 32–33; Martin Good/Shutterstock Images, pp. 4–5; Paul Sakuma/AP Images, pp. 40–41; PAUL VATHIS/AP Images, pp. 8–9; Rick Bowmer/AP Images, pp. 14–15; STEVE HELBER/AP Images, p. 31; Tony Dejak/AP Images, pp. 36–37; TY RUSSELL/AP Images, p. 29; Warren M. Winterbottom/AP Images, pp. 6–7
Design Elements: ayagiz/iStockphoto (hexagon texture); huseyintuncer/iStockphoto (turf); LeArchitecto/iStockphoto (lights); Roman Bykhalets/iStockphoto (dots)

LIBRARY OF CONGRESS CONTROL NUMBER: 2022940526

PUBLISHER'S CATALOGING-IN-PUBLICATION DATA

Names: Monnig, Alex, author.
Title: Basketball / by Alex Monnig
Description: Minneapolis, Minnesota : Abdo Publishing, 2023 | Series: Xtreme moments in sports | Includes online resources and index.
Identifiers: ISBN 9781532199288 (lib. bdg.) | ISBN 9781098274481 (ebook)
Subjects: LCSH: Basketball--Juvenile literature. | Basketball--History--Juvenile literature. | Sports--History--Juvenile literature.
Classification: DDC 796.323--dc23

TABLE OF CONTENTS

CHAPTER 1

BASKETBALL BEGINNINGS

Dr. James Naismith invented basketball in 1891. The hoops were peach baskets. The ball was a soccer ball. Over time, the game changed into the fast-paced sport of today. There have been many amazing basketball games and players.

Naismith was born in Almonte, Ontario, Canada. Today, the town features a statue of him.

Wilt Chamberlain was one of the most **dominant** NBA players of all time. On March 2, 1962, he was more unstoppable than ever. Chamberlain's Philadelphia Warriors were playing the New York Knicks. At halftime, Chamberlain had already scored 41 points. But he was just getting started.

Chamberlain (#13) was one of the first NBA players who was more than 7 feet (2.1 m) tall.

The Warriors players wanted to see how many points Chamberlain could score. So, they kept passing to him. With 46 seconds left in the game, Chamberlain scored his one hundredth point. It's a record many believe will never be broken.

After Chamberlain scored his one hundredth point, some fans ran onto the court to congratulate him.

XTREME FACT

Kobe Bryant of the Los Angeles Lakers has come closest to Chamberlain's record. He scored 81 points against the Toronto Raptors on January 22, 2006.

CHAPTER 3

REED STEPS UP

In 1970, the New York Knicks were playing the Los Angeles Lakers in the NBA **championships**. The series was tied 3-3 with one game left. Unfortunately, the Knicks had a problem. The team's captain and star player, Willis Reed, was injured. He had hurt his thigh in Game 5. He did not play in Game 6.

XTREME FACT

Reed played in the NBA All-Star game seven times. He was voted into the Naismith Memorial Basketball Hall of Fame in 1982.

Reed played for the Knicks from 1964 to 1974.

Reed and Knicks coach and manager Red Holzman holding the NBA Championship trophy

Nobody knew if Reed would be able to play in Game 7. Could the Knicks win without Reed? But moments before **tip-off**, he hobbled onto the court. The crowd went wild! Reed only scored a few points in the game. But his **determination** helped inspire the Knicks to a 113-99 victory. This gave the team its first NBA title!

CHAPTER 4
CHARLES DUNKS
TO VICTORY

It was the final game of the 1983 NCAA men's basketball **championship**. North Carolina (NC) State was playing the University of Houston. Houston was the top team in the country and had won 26 games in a row. So, almost everybody believed Houston would win.

University of Houston stars Hakeem Olajuwon (*left*) and Clyde Drexler (*right*) went on to become NBA Hall of Famers. They played together on the Houston Rockets from 1995 to 1998.

Whittenburg taking the shot that Charles caught and dunked

The score was tied with just seconds left. NC State's Dereck Whittenburg had the ball. He fired a shot from 30 feet (9.1 m) away. Teammate Lorenzo Charles was near the basket. He saw that Whittenburg's shot would miss.

Charles jumped and grabbed the ball in front of the rim. He **dunked** it with one second remaining. NC State won! It was one of the biggest upsets in basketball history.

Charles's game-winning dunk

CHAPTER 5

THE SHOT

On March 28, 1992, the University of Kentucky was playing Duke University in the 1992 NCAA tournament. It was a close game that went to overtime. With just 2.1 seconds left, Kentucky scored to take a one-point lead. It seemed sure that they would win.

Mike Krzyzewski was Duke's head coach from 1980 to 2022. He led Duke to five NCAA titles. He is one of the best basketball coaches in history.

Hill went on to play in the NBA for 19 years. He was voted into the Naismith Memorial Basketball Hall of Fame in 2018.

Laettner taking the game-winning shot

But Duke had one more chance. Grant Hill stood at the far end of the court to **inbound** the ball. He launched it toward teammate Christian Laettner. Laettner was at Duke's foul line. He caught the ball with his back to the basket. He turned and released the shot. It went in and Duke won the game!

CHAPTER 6

JORDAN GOES OUT ON TOP

It was June 14, 1998. The Chicago Bulls were playing the Utah Jazz in the NBA **playoffs**. The Bulls were losing 86-85 with 10 seconds left. Bulls' superstar Michael Jordan had the ball.

Jordan played for the Bulls from 1984 to 1993 and from 1995 to 1998.

Jazz player Bryon Russell was guarding Jordan. Jordan started to move to his right. Then he suddenly stopped, and Russell flew past him. Jordan rose up and released a jump shot just before the buzzer. *Swish!*

The Bulls won the game and the **championship**! It was the team's third consecutive title. Many people consider Jordan to be the greatest player ever. He led the Bulls to six championships in eight years. That game-winning shot was his last one as a Chicago Bull.

Jordan was the NBA Finals Most Valuable Player (MVP) for all six of the Bulls' **championship** seasons. He was also the team leader in points those seasons.

Jordan (*left*) received the NBA Finals MVP Award. Head coach Phil Jackson holds the NBA Championship trophy.

CHAPTER 7

PARKER DUNKS
TWICE

At the 2003-2004 Gatorade High School Players of the Year Awards, Parker was named National Girls Basketball Athlete of the Year.

Candace Parker is a basketball player known for her **dunks**. Dunking is less common in women's basketball than in men's. Parker wasn't the first woman to do it. But she was the first to dunk on live television during the NCAA women's basketball tournament.

In 2004, Parker won the slam dunk contest at the McDonald's All-American High School Team competition.

Parker takes a shot during the 2008 NCAA championship game against Stanford University.

XTREME FACT

Tennessee lost in the **quarterfinals** of the 2006 NCAA tournament. But the team later won back-to-back titles in 2007 and 2008.

In college, Parker played for the University of Tennessee. On March 19, 2006, Tennessee faced the United States Military **Academy** in the NCAA tournament. About seven minutes into the game, Parker got the ball at midcourt. She raced toward the hoop. She leaped up off her left foot and slammed the ball through the hoop with her right hand.

Parker's first dunk in the 2006 NCAA tournament

After college, Parker played for the Los Angeles Sparks and the Chicago Sky in the WNBA.

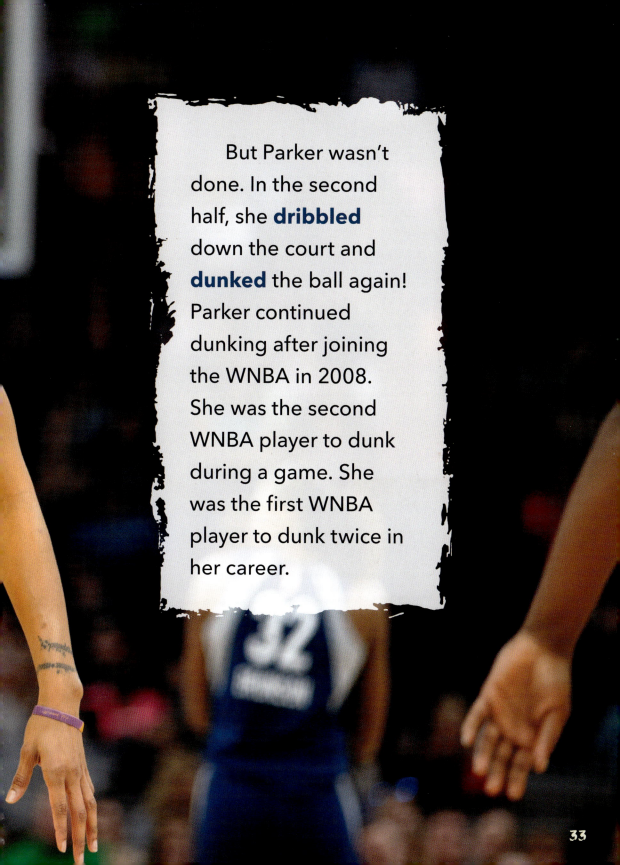

But Parker wasn't done. In the second half, she **dribbled** down the court and **dunked** the ball again! Parker continued dunking after joining the WNBA in 2008. She was the second WNBA player to dunk during a game. She was the first WNBA player to dunk twice in her career.

CHAPTER 8

THE BLOCK

LeBron James grew up near Cleveland, Ohio. He joined the Cleveland Cavaliers in 2003. James then moved to Florida's Miami Heat in 2010. He helped the Heat win NBA **championships** in 2012 and 2013.

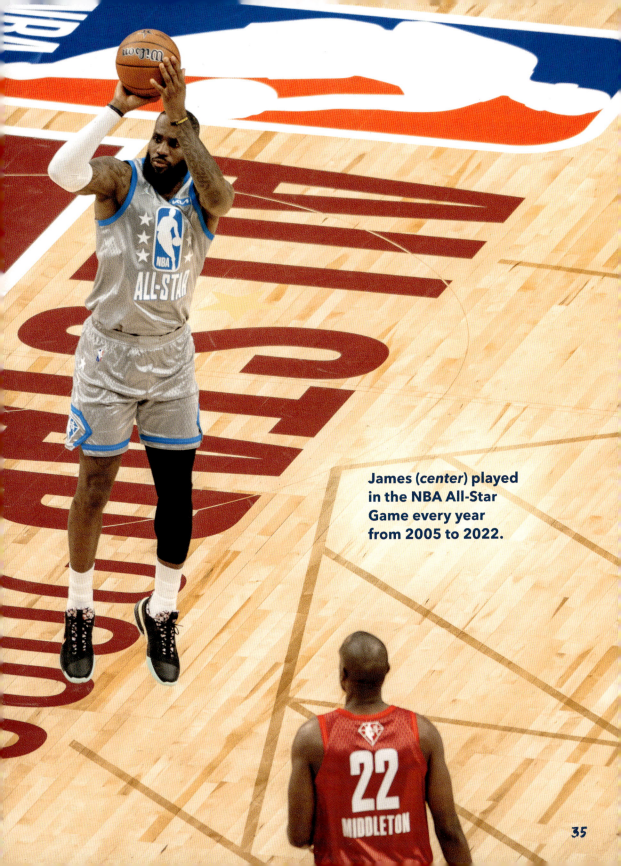

James (*center*) played in the NBA All-Star Game every year from 2005 to 2022.

James returned to the Cavaliers in 2014. That year, he led the team to the **playoffs**. But they lost to the Golden State Warriors in the finals. The two teams met in the finals again in 2016. James's scoring helped the Cavaliers tie the series 3–3. But he saved his best for last.

James (#23) scored 41 points in both Game 5 and Game 6.

James blocking Iguodala's shot in the final minutes of Game 7

Game 7 was tied 89-89 with less than two minutes left. Warriors **small forward** Andre Iguodala went for a **layup**. James soared through the air to swat the ball away. This play became known as "The Block." It helped the Cavaliers go on to win their first NBA title!

James holds the NBA championship trophy surrounded by his teammates. James also holds his NBA Finals MVP trophy.

CHAPTER 9

OGWUMIKE WINS
THE GAME

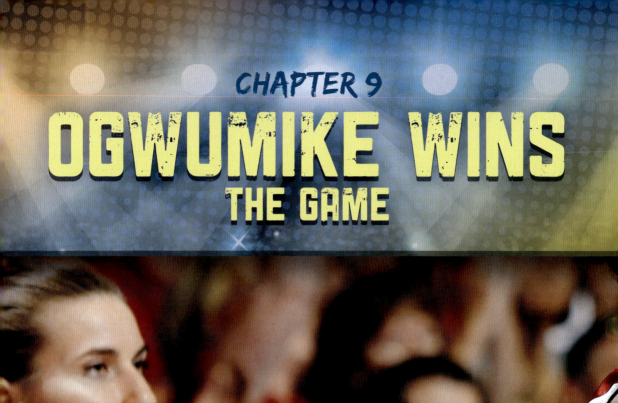

It was Game 5 of the 2016 WNBA finals between the Minnesota Lynx and Los Angeles Sparks. The Lynx were ahead by one point with 3.1 seconds left in the game. If they held on, they'd win their fourth WNBA title in six years.

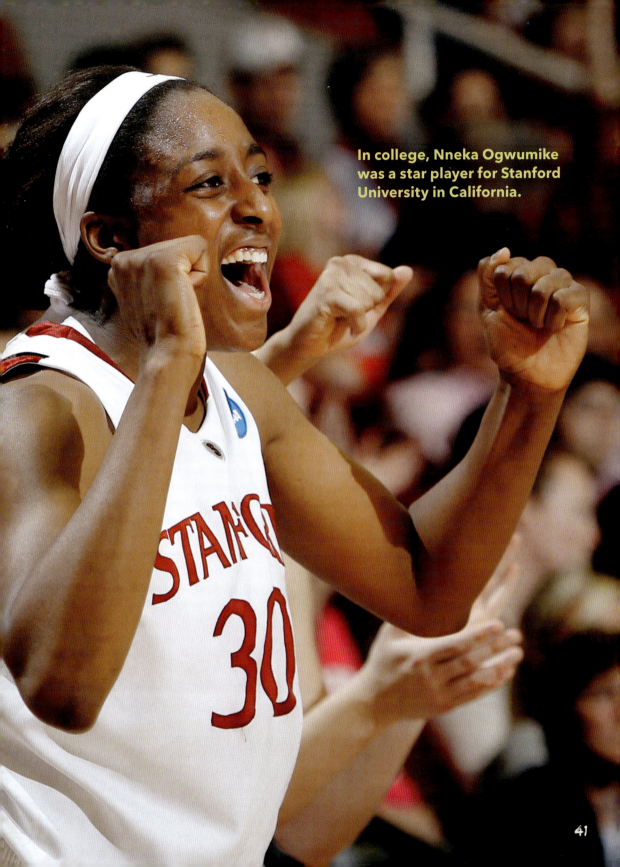

In college, Nneka Ogwumike was a star player for Stanford University in California.

Ogwumike's (*left*) game-winning shot

Ogwumike (#30) celebrates winning the title. She was later named WNBA MVP for the 2016 season.

The Sparks' Nneka Ogwumike had other ideas. She took a shot that was blocked. But she got the **rebound** with 3.1 seconds left. Falling backward, she released a desperate shot. The swish won the Sparks the WNBA **championship**.

CHAPTER 10

THE FUTURE
OF BASKETBALL

Basketball has been a favorite of sports fans for decades. Every season brings exciting new players and record-breaking games. Superstars such as Ja Morant, Giannis Antetokounmpo, and A'ja Wilson will continue to thrill fans and make memories on the court.

XTREME CHALLENGE

TAKE THE QUIZ BELOW AND
PUT WHAT YOU'VE LEARNED TO THE TEST!

1) How many points did Wilt Chamberlain score during the game on March 2, 1962?

2) What emotions do you think LeBron James felt when he returned to Cleveland and won a championship with his hometown team?

3) What other championships did Candace Parker win in her basketball career?

4) Who was guarding Michael Jordan when he hit his title-winning shot against the Utah Jazz in 1998?

5) Why do you think it was important for Willis Reed to play for the Knicks in Game 7 of the 1970 NBA Finals even though he only scored four points?

GLOSSARY

academy—a private high school. An academy is also a school that trains students in a certain field, such as the military.

championship—a game, a match, or a race held to find a first-place winner.

determination—a firm or fixed intention to succeed at something or complete a task.

dominant—being more powerful, successful, or important than all others.

dribble—to continually bounce a basketball with one hand.

dunk—in basketball, to jump up and push the ball down through the basket.

inbound—in basketball, when a player throws the ball to a teammate from out of bounds.

layup—a shot in basketball made from near the basket, usually by bouncing the ball off the backboard into the basket.

playoffs—a series of games to determine which team will win a championship.

quarterfinals—the round of a tournament that involves eight teams.

rebound—the act of gaining control of the basketball after a missed shot.

small forward—a position in basketball. The small forward is usually the team's best defensive player but is also a good shooter.

tip-off—the start of a basketball game when the referee tosses the ball up and a player from each team tries to hit it to a teammate.

ONLINE RESOURCES

Booklinks
NONFICTION NETWORK
FREE! ONLINE NONFICTION RESOURCES

To learn more about basketball, please visit **abdobooklinks.com** or scan this QR code. These links are routinely monitored and updated to provide the most current information available.

INDEX